What Is the Story of The Wizard of Oz?

What Is the Story of The Wizard of Oz?

by Kirsten Anderson

illustrated by Robert Squier

Penguin Workshop

To Pickwick, who left for Oz far too soon—KA

For Trish, the Good Witch of the West—RS

PENGUIN WORKSHOP
An Imprint of Penguin Random House LLC, New York

Published by Penguin Workshop,
an imprint of Penguin Random House LLC, New York. PENGUIN and PENGUIN WORKSHOP are trademarks of Penguin Books Ltd. WHO HQ & Design is a registered trademark of Penguin Random House LLC. Printed in the USA.

Visit us online at www.penguinrandomhouse.com.

Library of Congress Cataloging-in-Publication Data is available upon request.

ISBN 9781524788308 (paperback)   10 9 8 7 6 5 4 3 2 1
ISBN 9781524788315 (library binding)   10 9 8 7 6 5 4 3 2 1

Contents

What Is the Story of *The Wizard of Oz*?

The very high point—the moment everyone in the audience waits for—in one of the most popular musicals on Broadway comes as a young woman stands alone onstage. She begins singing about how tired she is of trying to do what others want her to do and be who they want her to be. It's time for her to believe in herself and to fight for what she thinks is right.

Many of the people in the audience share her struggle. They, too, want to believe in themselves, but may not have the confidence. They feel just like the young woman singing "Everyone deserves the chance to fly!"

And then she rises into the air and flies. And their spirits soar with her.

This isn't just any young woman. She has

green skin, wears a tall, pointy hat, and holds a broom. She is a witch—the evil witch who battled Dorothy in *The Wizard of Oz*.

But this is *Wicked*, the hit musical that tells the true story of Elphaba, the Wicked Witch of the West, and her friendship with Glinda the Good Witch. In this version, Elphaba is the star, and she

is not as "wicked" as she appeared in *The Wizard of Oz*. This is Elphaba's big moment, where she sings "Defying Gravity." The song and the flying are the high points of the show, and something audiences cheer every night.

Wicked opened on Broadway in 2003 and has been attracting huge crowds ever since. But

the story of Oz, the witches, Dorothy, and the Wizard goes back even further. Beyond the famous 1939 movie, where Dorothy is the hero who sings about finding a special place over the rainbow. Even earlier than 1900, when a book called *The Wonderful Wizard of Oz* was published and became a beloved classic.

It goes back to the 1800s. To a little boy with a big imagination, who had nightmares about being chased by a scarecrow.

CHAPTER 1
Frankie

Lyman Frank Baum was born on May 15, 1856, in Chittenango, New York. His parents were Benjamin and Cynthia Baum, and he had two sisters and two brothers. Frankie, as he was known, was lucky to survive. He was born in the middle of a diphtheria epidemic. Two of his cousins and his three-year-old brother had died from the disease (which is a very serious infection) right around the time Frankie was born. The Baums had another son, Henry, known as Harry, in 1859.

The Baums did not have much money when Frankie was very young. But then Benjamin started working in the oil business and became wealthy. In 1861, the family bought a mansion in the city of Syracuse. And five years later, the Baums moved to a grand estate called Rose Lawn, just outside of town.

In the fall of 1868, twelve-year-old Frankie was sent away to military school. He hated the rules and strict teachers. In 1870, he became sick at school and collapsed. His family took him home for good, which was fine with Frankie. He much preferred life at Rose Lawn, where he could read the fairy tales he loved, and daydream as much as he wanted.

Not all of his dreams were good, though. For a while, Frankie kept having the same nightmare. A scarecrow was chasing him through the fields around Rose Lawn. Just as it was about to catch him, it would collapse into a pile of straw and clothes. He never forgot that dream.

When Frankie was fourteen, his father bought him a small printing press. He and his brother Harry began to print the *Rose Lawn Home Journal*, a newspaper for the family. They wrote stories, news, and puzzles for it. Frankie also wrote poems and stories for himself, and even started a novel.

In 1873, a financial crisis struck the United States. All over the country, people lost money, businesses, and their homes. Benjamin Baum was deeply in debt and out of money. Seventeen-year-old Frankie had to drop out of school and go to work in a store owned by his older sister and her husband.

Frank did not like working in the store. He had always loved the theater, and in 1878, he decided to go to New York to become an actor. He got a few parts in plays, but wasn't earning enough to make a living. He left New York for Bradford, Pennsylvania, where he worked on a weekly journal.

Eventually, his father let him manage a group of theaters he still owned from his wealthier days, and Frank started his own theater company. In 1882, Frank wrote a play called *The Maid of Arran*. He also played the lead role. The play

was popular, and was performed around the East Coast and the Midwest.

That year, Frank married Maud Gage, a well-educated young woman.

Maud Gage on her wedding day

In 1883, Maud gave birth to their son Frank Joslyn. Frank wasn't making enough money with his theater company, so he went into business with his older brother Benjamin Jr. They sold a type of oil that helped machines run smoothly. Maud and Frank had another son, Robert Stanton, in 1886. Afterward, Maud had to spend months in bed. Frank took care of Frank Jr. and Robert, and became very close to his sons.

Frank and Benjamin's business wasn't doing well. Maud's brother Clarkson and sisters Julia and Helen had moved out west to the territory that would become North and South Dakota. Their letters to Maud made life in the West sound exciting. Maybe a little too exciting: Helen described a frightening cyclone that lifted a house right off the ground! Frank's business in Syracuse wasn't very successful. So in the fall of 1888, he decided to move his family to Aberdeen, South Dakota.

The Baum home in Aberdeen, South Dakota, 1888

CHAPTER 2
Aberdeen

Everything in South Dakota was much different from the life Frank knew back east. The Dakota prairie was flat and open, filled with empty land and big sky.

Aberdeen was a fast-growing town, though.

New people arrived all the time, and houses and businesses were popping up quickly. Frank decided to open a store. Baum's Bazaar sold fancy things like lamps, tea sets, gold pens, and gold toothpicks. For children, there were dolls, bicycles, and train sets.

At first the store was a success, but a drought struck the area in 1889. Crops didn't grow, and suddenly no one had money to buy much at all, let alone fancy china and gold toothpicks. The store closed on January 1, 1890.

Frank then started a newspaper called the *Aberdeen Saturday Pioneer*. The paper was popular, but the town was still struggling. The drought went on and on. Businesses failed and people left.

In 1891, the Baums moved to Chicago. Frank worked as a buyer for a department store, then as a traveling salesman for a glass and china company. He was often away from home.

Frank and Maud had two more sons, Harry and Ken. Frank loved the nights he could spend at home telling stories to his sons. When he was on the road, he wrote down ideas for new stories. He invented new lands and strange creatures who did magical things. He began to write stories and poems for adults, too.

In 1897, Frank published a book called *Mother Goose in Prose*. Frank's stories answered the questions his own children had asked about the Old Mother Goose rhymes, like why the old  woman who lived in a shoe had so many children.

Frank followed up his first book with another collection of stories called *Father Goose, His Book*. These stories and poems were similar to the old fairy tales he'd read as a child.

Children's Books in the Nineteenth Century

In the early 1800s, books of fairy tales by the Brothers Grimm were very popular, as were the stories of Hans Christian Andersen. Later writers were strongly influenced by fairy tales and began to create their own.

Alice's Adventures in Wonderland, written by Lewis Carroll and published in 1865, was one of the most popular children's books of its time. It wasn't a story about dragons, or castles, or lost fortunes, though. This was a child's book that went in a new direction: Imaginary talking animals and silly adults teased Alice with confusing rhymes and puzzles. The stories and the tone of the Alice books influenced many writers, including Frank Baum.

But Frank wanted to make them more modern. He wrote about kids flying through the sky in fantastic machines rather than fighting dragons.

A friend introduced Frank to an illustrator named W. W. Denslow, who was known for his funny, lively drawings. Frank showed some of his new stories to Denslow, and he agreed to illustrate *Father Goose*.

Father Goose was published in 1899. To Frank's surprise, it was a hit with both readers and critics. Suddenly he was a successful children's author.

But he didn't have much time to think about his success. He was busy finishing a new book. It was about a girl who is carried away to a strange new land. He named the land Oz.

W. W. Denslow (1856–1915)

William Wallace Denslow attended both the National Academy of Design and the Cooper Union in New York. Denslow, often called "Den," worked as an artist and newspaper reporter around the country until 1893, when he decided to settle in Chicago after visiting the world's fair. He was best known as a poster artist, but also illustrated books. He earned enough money as an artist to buy an island in Bermuda! There he crowned himself King Denslow I, Monarch of Denslow Islands and Protector of Coral Reefs.

CHAPTER 3
The Wonderful Wizard of Oz

The Wonderful Wizard of Oz tells the story of Dorothy, a little girl who lives on the dull, gray prairie of Kansas with her Aunt Em and Uncle Henry. One day a strong, rotating wind—called a cyclone—picks up their house and carries it away, with Dorothy and her dog, Toto, still inside! The house drops down in Munchkinland, a beautiful place where the grass is green and flowers are blooming. Dorothy is cheered by the Munchkins because the house landed on their enemy—the Wicked Witch of the East.

The Good Witch of the North arrives and tells Dorothy she should take the Wicked Witch's silver slippers, as they are very powerful. When Dorothy asks which way is the road back to Kansas, the Good Witch tells her to follow the yellow brick road to the Emerald City. There, the

Wizard of Oz might be able to help her. She gives Dorothy a kiss. And that kiss leaves a small mark to show that the Good Witch is protecting her.

Dorothy and Toto set off, and along the way they meet a scarecrow who wants brains, a tin man who is looking for a heart, and a lion who wants to become more courageous. They join her in the hope that the Wizard might be able to grant their requests. They battle fierce tiger-bears called Kalidahs, escape a field of deadly poppy flowers, then finally make it to the Emerald City.

The Wizard appears in different shapes to each of them and tells them he will help them if they kill the Wicked Witch of the West. She is the sister of the witch whom Dorothy's house landed on back in Munchkinland. The worried friends set off to find her, but the Wicked Witch sees them coming and sends her Winged Monkeys after them. The monkeys injure the Scarecrow and the Tin Woodman. They capture Dorothy, Toto, and the Lion.

The Wicked Witch sees the Good Witch's mark on Dorothy and realizes she can't hurt her. But she does try to steal the silver slippers. Dorothy becomes angry and throws a bucket of water at the Witch. To her surprise, the Witch melts.

Dorothy frees the Lion and the enslaved Winkie people. She is reunited with the Scarecrow and Tin Woodman, and the group of friends return to the Emerald City.

The Wizard of Oz is now invisible. The friends speak up, telling the Wizard that they killed the Wicked Witch of the West and asking him to grant their wishes. He tells them to come back the next day. While they argue with him about when he will keep his promise, Toto runs to the back of the room. He knocks over a screen and reveals a frightened little old man. He admits that he is actually the Wizard.

He arrived in Oz when the hot-air balloon he was riding in for a circus act in Omaha blew away. The people of Oz assumed he was a wizard, and he continued to use some of his circus tricks to keep them believing he was magical.

The Wizard decides to fly his balloon back to the United States with Dorothy. But, in a cruel twist, he accidentally lifts off without her. Dorothy is crushed, thinking she will never get home. Then an Oz soldier suggests that she visit Glinda, the Good Witch of the South.

Glinda explains to Dorothy that all she ever needed to get back to Kansas were her silver slippers. Dorothy says goodbye to her friends, then, holding on to Toto, takes three steps. Dorothy whirls away and lands back in Kansas, where she finds Aunt Em. And Dorothy tells her how glad she is to be back home.

The Geography of Oz

The country of Oz is roughly shaped like a rectangle and divided into four parts. To the east is Munchkinland, and to the west is the land of the Winkies. The Quadlings live in the south and the Gillikins in the north. The Emerald City is in the very center of the country.

The people in each region are represented by one specific color. Their clothes and anything they make is that color. The Munchkins' color is blue; the color of the Winkies is yellow. The Quadlings live in the land of red, and the Gillikins in the land of purple. And, of course, the Emerald City is green.

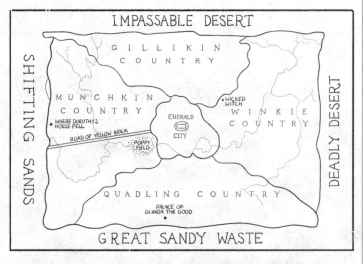

The map of Oz shows East on the left and West on the right.

Frank had started out wanting to create a fairy tale like the ones he had loved when he was young. But his was an American fairy tale, based on the America Frank knew. The dull, gray prairie where Dorothy lives was like Aberdeen, South Dakota, during the drought. The Munchkins' rich,

New York City, 1890s

blooming farmland was the prairie and Midwest at its best, full of growth and opportunity. The deep forest Dorothy and her friends cross was like the ones Frank played in as a boy in upstate New York. The Emerald City was as dazzling as any of the cities growing quickly across the United States.

And the creatures Dorothy met were not elves or fairies, but everyday things: a scarecrow, something made of tin, and an animal.

And Dorothy felt familiar, too. She wasn't a princess stuck in a castle. She was an American girl who relied on herself, like the people who went out west and tried to make a new life on the prairie. Like them, she solved her own problems and stood up for herself. When she saw someone in need, like the Scarecrow, Tin Woodman, or the Cowardly Lion, she helped them—just the way someone in Kansas or South Dakota or Pennsylvania might help their neighbor. After seeing exotic, beautiful places with gleaming cities and roads made of gold, she still just wanted to go home to Kansas.

The Wonderful Wizard of Oz was published in May 1900. The *New York Times* said it was "a book that rises far above the average children's book of today," and praised its "bright and joyous atmosphere." The reviewer thought that it would "be strange if there be a normal child who will not enjoy the story."

And the reviewer was right. By Christmas 1900 the book was a best seller.

CHAPTER 4
The Royal Historian of Oz

A theater producer in Chicago decided to turn *The Wonderful Wizard of Oz* into a musical. The play was very different from the book, though. In the stage version, Dorothy was a teenager with a pet cow named Imogene. She traveled to Oz

with a waitress named Trixie! There was a large chorus of singing and dancing girls, fancy sets, and impressive special effects. The Scarecrow and Tin Woodman were played by a popular comedy team who did a lot of clowning around. But when *The Wizard of Oz* opened in June 1902, audiences loved it. The production toured North America for about eight years.

Frank earned a lot of money from the success of the musical and the sales of his book, but he spent more than he made. He decided to write a sequel to *The Wonderful Wizard of Oz*. Frank and W. W. Denslow had argued about profits from the *Oz* stage musical and didn't want to work together anymore. The new book was illustrated by a different artist, John R. Neill.

The Marvelous Land of Oz was published in 1904 and became another big best seller. Children had been waiting anxiously for more stories about the land of Oz. Frank hoped that he could turn it into another successful musical. He wrote the script himself and named it *The Woggle-Bug*, after the most popular character in the new book. It opened in June 1905 and was a huge flop.

Frank knew that nothing he wrote was as successful as the Oz books. And although he didn't want to write more about Oz, he needed the money. *Ozma of Oz* was published in 1907, and *Dorothy and the Wizard in Oz* in 1908. He called himself the Royal Historian of Oz.

The Road to Oz was published in 1909, and *The Emerald City of Oz* in 1910—a book that Frank thought would be his last Oz book.

Frank and Maud moved to California. To help pay off some of his debts, Frank signed over the copyrights—the legal right to publish—to his early books, including *The Wonderful Wizard of Oz*. That meant he would not earn any more money from his most famous book.

Frank wrote other stories that were not about Oz or the original characters. But readers just wanted more Oz. And Frank needed to earn a living, so he went back to writing about Oz.

The Patchwork Girl of Oz was published in 1913. It was about Scraps, a fun-loving "patchwork" girl quilted together from old pieces of cloth. It was Frank's best-selling book in years.

The Interesting Characters of Oz

With each book, Frank introduced a few new characters. Here are three of the most famous:

Scraps

Scraps, the Patchwork Girl, is a teenage girl sewn together from scraps of cloth. Her hair is brown yarn, her eyes are buttons, and her teeth are made from pearls. She is known for her enthusiasm and love of dancing and jumping around.

Tik-Tok is a mechanical man. He is built like a windup toy, with three keys: one for thinking, one for speaking, and one for moving. Each key needs to be wound in

Tik-Tok

order for him to function completely.

The Woggle-Bug is an ordinary insect who lives in a schoolhouse, so he is very smart. He becomes human-size during a schoolroom experiment that goes wrong.

Woggle-Bug

CHAPTER 5
A New Historian

In 1914, Frank and three friends formed the Oz Film Manufacturing Company. They built a huge studio and made three films, *The Patchwork Girl of Oz*, *The Magic Cloak of Oz*, and *His Majesty, the Scarecrow of Oz*.

Frank worked very hard on the films, spending long days and nights at the studio. He helped with the building of the sets and invented special effects that created a magical world. Everything about the movies was of the highest quality.

But the films failed. At that time, no one made films just for children. Adults who went to the

Oz movies were disappointed that they had paid to see what they considered to be a simple fairy tale. Many demanded their money back. Theaters refused to show the films.

The failure of the films upset Frank deeply. He had put so much effort into them and was very proud of them. He gave up on film and theater. From now on, he would just write his books and tend the flowers he loved in his garden.

Between 1915 and 1919, Frank wrote five more Oz books. His heart weakened and he died on May 6, 1919. He was sixty-two years old. He left behind manuscripts for two more Oz books. *The Magic of Oz* was published in 1919, and *Glinda of Oz* came out in 1920.

Reilly & Lee, the books' publisher, didn't want the series to end, though. They decided to find a new writer to take over and become the next Royal Historian of Oz. William F. Lee, the vice president of the company, noticed the stories of

a writer named Ruth Plumly Thompson on the children's page of a Philadelphia newspaper. He thought they were very imaginative and written in a lively, fun style. Reilly & Lee offered Ruth Thompson

Ruth Plumly Thompson

a contract to write one new Oz book a year.

Ruth had grown up reading the Oz books and was thrilled by the offer. She accepted, and her first book, *The Royal Book of Oz*, was published in 1921. She went on to write eighteen more Oz books! Like Frank, she enjoyed creating new, fun characters. She invented Pigasus, the flying pig who loved poetry; Reachard, who had an arm that could stretch to reach anything; and Sir Hokus of Pokes, an elderly knight from

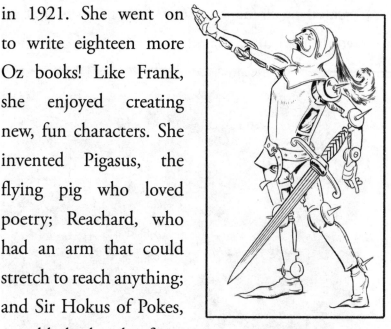

Sir Hokus of Pokes

the time of King Arthur who was still ready to fight dragons.

Kids loved Ruth's new books, and she wrote one a year until 1939. But then she didn't write any more Oz books until the 1970s.

Yet Oz became more and more popular throughout the rest of the twentieth century and into the twenty-first. The land and characters created by Frank won new fans in ways that he would have appreciated: on-screen and onstage.

CHAPTER 6
Oz and the Silver Screen

In the 1910s and 1920s, movies were in black and white. And they didn't have a soundtrack. They were silent. Actors pretended to speak, but audiences couldn't hear them. Instead, they watched the expressions on the actors' faces, and their gestures, to try to understand the story. Sometimes title cards with words on them appeared on-screen. They showed the most

'Marry you – an aristo-crat! Why, that would ruin you in the eyes of all the world!

important parts of the conversations, or gave details that audiences might not figure out on their own.

In 1925, there was a new movie version of *The Wizard of Oz*. Like the other Oz plays and movies, the plot was very different from the book. And like the other Oz films, this one also was a failure. It seemed that no one could get the Oz story quite right when making a movie about it.

Silent movies began to disappear after 1927 when *The Jazz Singer* was released, a movie with recorded sound! Soon, studios were making all kinds of "talking pictures," including musicals with lots of singing and dancing. They still weren't interested in children's movies or fairy tales, though.

But in 1937, a movie came along that made everyone change their minds about fairy-tale films. It was *Snow White*, Disney's animated version of the classic story. To everyone's surprise, it was a huge hit. Suddenly, all the big movie studios began to look for fairy tales and children's stories that they could turn into their own *Snow White*–size hits.

Five different studios offered to buy the rights to *The Wonderful Wizard of Oz* from producer Sam Goldwyn, who had bought them from the Baum family a few years earlier. He sold it to the highest bidder, Metro-Goldwyn-Mayer (MGM), for $75,000 in 1938. MGM's motto was "All the stars there are in heaven," and the studio bragged about having the biggest stars in Hollywood under contract.

Not-So-Silent Films

Silent films weren't always silent! Many of them were shown with live music.

In the early 1900s, theaters began to hire piano players or organists to play during movies, mostly to cover up the sound from the noisy film projectors. At first, the musicians just played whatever they wanted.

But filmmakers soon realized that music could be used to help tell the story. It could make a chase scene more exciting, or make a love scene more romantic. They hired composers to write music especially for the movies. The movie reels would arrive at the theater with a set of sheet music and a list of musical cues telling the piano player what and when to play. The movies themselves may have been "silent," but, thanks to local musicians, they were never dull.

Today, an actor, writer, director, or crew member will sign a contract to make a single movie. But in the 1930s and 1940s, most people signed a long-term contract with a studio. The studios always had numerous movies in production. When actors finished one film, they often went straight into preparing for another. Meanwhile, set designers, carpenters, seamstresses, and musicians worked nonstop, creating everything that was needed to

make many movies at a time. By the late 1930s, MGM was completing one movie every nine days.

MGM was one of the biggest and best studios in Hollywood. When they got the rights to *The Wonderful Wizard of Oz*, there was no question that it would be another spectacular MGM hit. It was—but there were a lot of bumps in the yellow brick road along the way.

CHAPTER 7
We're Off to See the Wizard

MGM decided that *The Wizard of Oz* would be a musical, with plenty of singing and dancing. And it would be in color! In 1938, color movies were still very new and exciting.

Some executives at MGM wanted Shirley Temple to play Dorothy. Ten-year-old Shirley

Shirley Temple

had been one of the biggest stars of the 1930s. The executives thought she would help make the movie a hit. But Shirley was under contract to another studio, and they would not loan her to MGM.

Instead, the role of Dorothy went to sixteen-year-old Judy Garland. She had been at MGM since 1935, but had been in only a few films. Many people at the studio didn't think

Judy Garland

she looked like the other glamorous MGM stars.

However, Judy had an amazing singing voice. People in the music department at MGM knew she was special. They thought the role of Dorothy would be a chance to show everyone what Judy could do, and that getting the role could help turn her into a star.

Judy Garland (1922–1969)

Frances Ethel Gumm sang onstage for the first time when she was just two and a half years old. After that, she began to perform with her older sisters as an act called the Gumm Sisters. In 1934, the girls changed their name to the Garland Sisters. Soon afterward, Frances changed her name to Judy.

After appearing in *The Wizard of Oz* in 1939, Judy became one of the studio's biggest stars. But she struggled with a dependence on drugs and alcohol. She began to show up late to film sets or not show up at all. Before she was thirty years old, MGM ended her contract.

Judy continued to make movies, but she really became a new kind of star, singing on the concert stage. Her shows were an event. People lined up in the streets to buy tickets, and the crowds cheered for her throughout her performances. The biggest

moment of each show was when Judy sang "Over
the Rainbow"—her special song from the movie
that had made her famous.

The casting department assigned the role of the Tin Man to Ray Bolger, an outstanding dancer who had starred in Broadway musicals. The role of the Scarecrow went to Buddy Ebsen, a tall, skinny young actor. Bolger was disappointed. He had always hoped to play the Scarecrow in a production of *The Wizard of Oz*. He kept pushing the casting department and, finally, they switched the actors' roles. Bert Lahr, a successful stage comedian, got the role of the Cowardly Lion.

Jack Haley, Bert Lahr, and Ray Bolger

At least eleven screenwriters worked on the script. One suggested that the Kansas scenes be filmed in black and white and the Oz scenes in color. Another invented Miss Gulch, a mean woman who wants to take Toto from Dorothy. Two writers took a line from the book and made it the theme of the whole movie: "There's no place like home."

Filming began on October 12, 1938. Nine days later, Buddy Ebsen, the Tin Man, became very sick and had to be hospitalized. He had had an allergic reaction to the aluminum dust that was used to make his face silver to look like tin. An actor named Jack Haley took over the role.

It took about two hours each morning for Bolger, Haley, and Lahr to be transformed into the Scarecrow, Tin Man, and Cowardly Lion. Bolger's rubber mask, and Haley's and Lahr's makeup, were so dense that their skin couldn't breathe. Lahr's lion costume weighed ninety pounds!

The Book Versus the Movie

Books often get changed when they are made into movies. Here are some differences between *The Wonderful Wizard of Oz*, the book, and *The Wizard of Oz*, the movie:

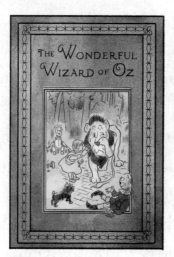 

Book	Movie
Dorothy is six years old.	Dorothy is twelve years old.
There are two good witches: the Good Witch of the North, and Glinda, the Good Witch of the South.	There is only one good witch, Glinda, and she is from the North.
The Wicked Witch of the East's slippers are silver.	The Wicked Witch of the East's slippers are ruby red because MGM thought red slippers would look better in color.
After the Wizard flies away, Dorothy and her friends have to travel to the South to get Glinda's help.	After the Wizard flies away, Glinda appears in the Emerald City and tells Dorothy how to get home.
Dorothy traveled to Oz.	Dorothy dreamed that she traveled to Oz.

Margaret Hamilton, the actress who played the Wicked Witch of the West, had her face and hands covered in thick green makeup. All of them were very uncomfortable. And Hamilton's skin stayed tinted green for months after the filming ended.

On the movie set, the lights necessary for the production made working under them brutally hot. When director Victor Fleming ordered all the lights turned off and the doors to the studio opened, everyone rushed out as fast as they could to get some fresh, cool air.

The set could be a dangerous place, too. Margaret Hamilton was severely burned during the filming of one of her scenes. She didn't return to work for six weeks. Her stuntwoman was injured in another scene and spent eleven days in the hospital.

Several Winged Monkeys were hurt when the wires that helped them to fly broke. An extra

stepped on Terry, the dog who played Toto, and sprained her paw. Jack Haley got an eye infection from his makeup and missed a few days of work.

Meanwhile, the craft departments at MGM were busy constructing a magical Oz. In 1939, there weren't any computers to create digital backgrounds or special effects. Everything had to be made by hand. The special effects department made the cyclone out of a giant piece of cloth wrapped around chicken wire. Wind machines made it swirl around as a car on tracks beneath the soundstage towed it along. To show Dorothy's house being lifted off the ground, the department built a miniature version of the whole farm. They filmed the tiny house being dropped to the ground, then ran the film backward to make it look like it was rising into the air. *The Wizard of Oz* finished filming on March 16, 1939.

Although it usually took eight weeks, at the most, for MGM to make a movie, it had taken

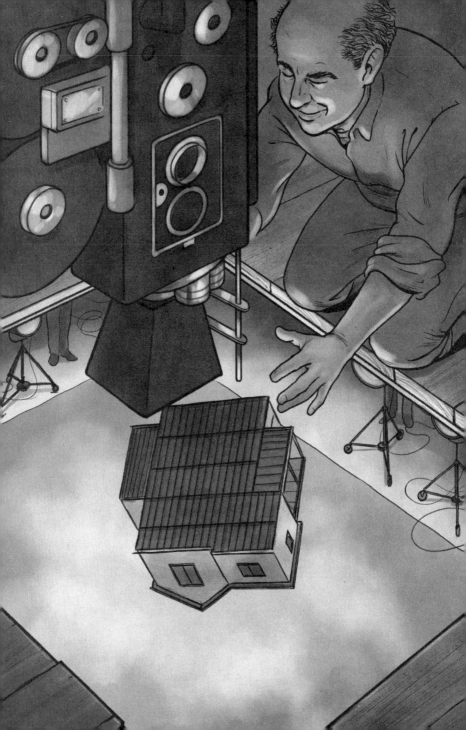

twenty-two weeks to film *Oz* and cost nearly $3 million—a huge amount in 1939. Some MGM executives thought the movie was too long and wanted to cut the song "Over the Rainbow," but the songwriter fought hard to keep it in the movie.

The Wizard of Oz opened nationally on August 25, 1939. Many critics thought it was just silly, or perhaps too sweet. Since it had been so expensive to make, it lost money for the studio by not earning enough in theaters.

The movie did win two Academy Awards that season, for best musical score and for "Over the Rainbow" as best original song. MGM had hoped the splashy color production would win more.

At the time, *The Wizard of Oz* was not a big hit.

But not too long afterward, a new kind of technology would let audiences see the movie in a whole new way. In 1939, the first televisions became available to the public. By 1951, the number of televisions in

Television from the 1950s

American households had grown to twelve million! In 1955, over half of American households had a television set. Television had become a part of American life.

CHAPTER 8
Ease on Down the Road

In 1956, the CBS television network bought the rights to show *The Wizard of Oz* on TV for the first time. CBS then decided to run the movie once every few years. Its ratings grew and grew, and at-home viewings became family events. A whole new generation of children and adults discovered

the movie and fell in love with Oz. By the early 1970s, the movie had become a beloved classic. Nearly forty years after it was shown in theaters, kids were learning the songs and the most famous lines from the movie by heart. Everyone seemed to have a favorite scene or character.

In 1972, a former radio host named Ken Harper had an idea. He decided to turn *The Wizard of Oz* into a stage musical with soul music and an all-black cast of actors. William F. Brown wrote the script for the musical, called *The Wiz*, and Charlie Smalls wrote most of the songs.

The Wiz is more similar to Frank Baum's original book than the 1939 movie was. The slippers are silver, not red. Dorothy has to take another long journey to get help from Glinda, and Dorothy's trip to Oz is not a dream.

Musicals and plays often tour in other cities before coming to New York. *The Wiz* opened at the Morris A. Mechanic Theatre in Baltimore, Maryland, on October 21, 1974. It didn't go very well, and the producers made a lot of changes. When *The Wiz* opened at the Majestic Theatre

on Broadway on January 5, 1975, it had replaced some cast members. Stephanie Mills played Dorothy, with Hinton Battle as the Scarecrow, Tiger Haynes as the Tin Man, Ted Ross as the Lion, Mabel King as Evillene, the Wicked Witch of the West, and André De Shields as the Wiz.

Original cast of *The Wiz*

It was unusual for Broadway shows to advertise on TV in the early 1970s. But Ken Harper made a commercial showing Dorothy, the Scarecrow, the Tin Man, and the Lion singing as they danced down the Yellow Brick Road. They sang a song called "Ease on Down the Road"—the updated version of "Follow the Yellow Brick Road." The commercial and the catchy song got people's attention. They began to buy tickets. Two weeks later, the show was selling out. Within a few weeks, it was one of Broadway's biggest hits.

The Wiz won seven Tony Awards in 1975, including Broadway's highest honor, best musical. The show ran for four years that included 1,672 performances.

Stephanie Mills

Stephanie Mills was born on March 22, 1957, in Brooklyn, New York. She first started singing at church, and made her Broadway debut in 1968. When she was eleven years old, she won Amateur Night at the Apollo Theater for six straight weeks. She went on to become the opening act for the Isley Brothers, one of the most popular singing groups at the time.

In the years after *The Wiz*, she had many hits, including "Two Hearts" and "What Cha Gonna Do With My Lovin'."

In 1980, she won a Grammy for best female rhythm and blues performance for the song "Never Knew Love Like This Before"—the biggest hit of her career.

In 1977, producers began to make *The Wiz* into a movie. Diana Ross, one of the biggest music stars in the world, wanted to play Dorothy, but she was thirty-three years old! The script was rewritten, and Dorothy became a schoolteacher in New York City. Oz was a dreamlike version of the city. Ted Ross, from the Broadway cast, played the Lion, and Nipsey Russell played the Tin Man. Comedian Richard Pryor played the Wiz. The Scarecrow was played by Michael Jackson, who

Richard Pryor

had become famous as a member of the family singing group the Jackson 5. This was his first movie role.

The Wiz has been performed all around the world and continues to be a popular musical today.

Original cast of *The Wiz* movie

Diana Ross

Diana Ross was born on March 26, 1944, in Detroit, Michigan. In her teens, she began singing with an all-female group called the Primettes. They got the attention of Motown Records executive Berry Gordy, who advised them to change their name. They became the Supremes, and Motown signed them to a contract in 1962. The Supremes were one of the biggest musical acts of the 1960s, with twelve number one hits, including "Where Did

Our Love Go," "Stop! In the Name of Love," and "You Can't Hurry Love."

Diana Ross left the Supremes in 1970 and launched a successful solo career. She also won acclaim as an actor for her performances in the movies *Lady Sings the Blues* and *Mahogany*.

She continued to perform and record throughout the 1980s, 1990s, and into the 2000s. She is known for her exciting live shows.

The Supremes

CHAPTER 9
Being Wicked

By the 1990s, it had been over fifty years since the 1939 movie was released, and twenty since *The Wiz* first appeared on Broadway. It was time to take a different look at L. Frank Baum's story.

In 1996, composer Stephen Schwartz heard  about a book called *Wicked: The Life and Times of the Wicked Witch of the West* by Gregory Maguire. Schwartz, who had written the music for the hit Broadway shows *Pippin* and *Godspell*, read the book and thought it would make a good musical.

Wicked opened at the Curran Theatre in San

Francisco on May 28, 2003, and had its Broadway premiere later that same year at the Gershwin Theatre in New York City. Idina Menzel starred as Elphaba, the Wicked Witch of the West, with Kristin Chenoweth as Glinda the Good Witch.

Wicked follows the story of Gregory Maguire's book. It begins with awkward, green-skinned Elphaba meeting the pretty, confident Galinda (later Glinda) at Shiz University. At first the girls are rivals, but eventually they become friends.

Elphaba's magical powers are quickly recognized, and she is given a chance to meet the Wizard of Oz. She is eager to see him because she wants to complain to him about how the talking animals, including her favorite professor, are being treated unfairly. Then she finds out that the Wizard is the one behind the plot against the animals.

Elphaba vows to fight against the Wizard, even though Glinda warns her not to. The Wizard tells people she is "wicked" in order to protect himself.

Elphaba goes off on her own, leaving her true love, Fiyero, behind. Glinda stays and works for the Wizard, and is considered to be the "good" character.

Years later, Elphaba and Fiyero are reunited. Glinda and Elphaba also meet again, and remember how much their friendship meant to them. Glinda tries to warn Elphaba that Dorothy is on her way. But she is too late and watches in horror as Dorothy melts Elphaba with a bucket of water. Fiyero arrives to open a trapdoor in

the floor. Elphaba steps out. Now that everyone thinks she is dead, the two of them can live secretly together in peace.

Wicked became a hit, selling out every night. Fans came to see it over and over. They bought the original cast recording and learned the songs.

It's Not Easy Being Green

Before every performance of *Wicked*, the actor playing Elphaba has to "go green." The makeup artist covers her face, neck, and ears in a makeup called Chromacake in Landscape Green. Powder is dusted on her face to help the makeup set and stay

on during the show. The artist also applies purple eye shadow and dark lipstick. For scenes where Elphaba wears a dress with short sleeves, she also wears a green leotard that covers her arms to her wrists. Then her hands are painted green, as well.

When *Wicked* became popular, MAC, the company that makes the green makeup, began to sell it to the public, so fans of the show could be "Elphaba green," too!

For many people, a chance to see *Wicked* was the highlight of a trip to New York City. The show's messages about friendship, being yourself, and the idea that you are worth being loved no matter who you are or what you look like meant a lot to audiences who came from all over the world to see it.

By April 2018, *Wicked* was the seventh-longest-running Broadway musical ever, with over six thousand performances. It had earned over $1 billion on Broadway and over $4.5 billion in worldwide touring shows. *Wicked* has helped keep the story of *The Wonderful Wizard of Oz* alive in the twenty-first century.

CHAPTER 10
The Magic of Oz

It's been more than one hundred years since L. Frank Baum wrote his story about the little girl whose house was carried away to a magical land on the winds of a cyclone. But readers still enjoy the tale, along with all the other Oz books. *The Wonderful Wizard of Oz* has been published in more than fifty languages. The International Wizard of Oz Club—for fans of all things Oz-related—was founded in 1957 and has members all around the world.

Superfans collect Oz items, like original copies of the books or promotional material from the plays, musicals, and movies. But costumes and props—all the items used on the set by the actors—from the 1939 movie are the most valuable items.

When the MGM movie finished filming, a crew member gave Ray Bolger his Scarecrow costume. Jack Haley's Tin Man costume was destroyed. Most of the other items were packed away in studio warehouses.

Once people became interested in the history of movies, the items seemed more valuable. When the MGM studio property was sold in 1970, many of the props and costumes that had been packed away for decades were auctioned off.

There were pieces from many classic MGM movies at the auction, but the *Oz* items got the most attention. The yearly TV showings had made *The Wizard of Oz* an annual event in many people's childhoods. One of the Cowardly Lion costumes, probably worn by a stuntman, sold for $2,400. Dorothy's ruby slippers sold for $15,000! No one had expected them to be so highly valued.

And prices for *Oz* items climbed even higher over the next few decades. The same lion costume from the 1970 auction sold for $826,000 in 2006.

In the 1990s, a lion costume that was probably worn by Bert Lahr was discovered on the MGM lot. It was in terrible condition, but James Comisar, a movie and TV collector, carefully

James Comisar with Bert Lahr's Cowardly Lion costume

restored it. And in 2014, someone bought it for more than $3 million!

Because costume departments often make several copies of costumes, there always had been more than one pair of ruby slippers. One pair belonged to a woman in Tennessee who had won them in a publicity contest in 1940. She sold her pair in 1988 for $165,000.

A member of the costume department at MGM had sold several pairs before 1980. Another pair was stolen while on loan to the Judy Garland Museum in Grand Rapids, Minnesota. The shoes were found thirteen years later, in 2018, with the help of the FBI's Minneapolis division.

The person who bought the pair sold at the 1970 auction donated them to the Smithsonian Institution's National Museum of American History in 1979. They became one of the museum's most popular exhibits, with millions of people stopping to look at them every year.

Over time, though, the famous red-sequined shoes needed to be preserved. The Smithsonian raised almost $350,000 from people around the world to restore the shoes.

Wonderful Words

Some of the most famous movie quotes in history come from the 1939 MGM movie *The Wizard of Oz*:

- Toto, I've a feeling we're not in Kansas anymore.
- I'll get you, my pretty, and your little dog, too!
- Lions, and tigers, and bears! Oh my!
- Be gone, before somebody drops a house on you, too!
- I'm melting!
- Pay no attention to that man behind the curtain.
- There's no place like home.

That's how much the story of *The Wizard of Oz* means to fans! Most people recognize a bit of Baum's story, even if they haven't read the book or seen the entire movie. Advertisers, artists, and writers can use a quote or image from the film and be sure the audience will understand their meaning.

The messages of *The Wizard of Oz* are simple, but timeless. Written over one hundred years ago, they still have meaning today. Good friends can get you through tough times. Life can be a journey full of hurdles and stumbling blocks, but ones that can certainly be overcome. There is no place like home, but there are also magical places over the rainbow waiting to be explored.

And maybe sometimes they can be the same place. After all, in the books of L. Frank Baum, eventually Dorothy did leave Kansas and move to Oz.

Bibliography

*Books for young readers

Culwell-Block, Logan. "*The Wizard of Oz, Wicked*, and *The Wiz*: Three Takes on an American Classic." *Playbill*, December 4, 2015.

De Giere, Carol. *Defying Gravity: The Creative Career of Stephen Schwartz, from Godspell to Wicked.* New York: Applause Theatre & Cinema Books, 2008.

Dowling, Colette. "How *The Wiz* Went from Nearly Closing on Opening Night to Becoming a Tony-Winning Hit—Here's What Happened in 1975." *Playbill*, May 24, 2015.

Evans, Erin E. "12 Things You May Not Have Known About *The Wiz*." *The Root*, December 1, 2015. https://www.theroot.com/12-things-you-may-not-have-known-about-the-wiz-1790861920.

Greene, David L., and Dick Martin. *The Oz Scrapbook.* New York: Random House, 1977.

Harmetz, Aljean. *The Making of the Wizard of Oz.* Chicago: Chicago Review Press, 2013.

Liptak, Andrew. "L. Frank Baum's Wonderful Land of Oz." *Kirkus Reviews*, May 22, 2014.

Loncraine, Rebecca. *The Real Wizard of Oz: The Life and Times of L. Frank Baum.* New York: Gotham Books, 2009.

Miller, Stuart. "Old Pelt for Sale: The Original Cowardly Lion," *The Wall Street Journal*, November 19, 2014.

O'Connell, Michael. "Leonardo DiCaprio Helps Buy Dorothy's Ruby Slippers for Academy of Motion Picture Arts & Sciences." *The Hollywood Reporter*, February 22, 2012.

Schwartz, Stephen. "*Wicked* History Part I." **Stephen Schwartz.** http://www.musicalschwartz.com/wicked-history.htm.

Stackpole, Thomas. "How Dorothy's Ruby Slippers Came to the Smithsonian." *Smithsonian Magazine*, November 16, 2016.